A Guide to True Peace

or

A Method of Attaining to Inward and Spiritual Prayer

The 1815 Edition

Compiled chiefly from the writings
of Archbishop Fenelon, Madam
Guyon, & Miguel Molinos, by
William Backhouse & James Janson

Introduction by Jim Wilson

Copyright Information

This is a resetting of the 1815 edition of 'A Guide to True Peace' which is in the public domain.

The 'Introduction' by Jim Wilson is original. People are free to quote from it as long as attribution is given, along with information as to how to obtain this publication.

Table of Contents

Page

Introduction by Jim Wilson 4
Acknowledgements 9
A Guide to True Peace 10
Preface 11
1: The Spirit of God
   Dwells in the Heart of Man 13
2: On Faith 17
3: On Prayer 20
4: All are Capable of Attaining to
   Inward, and Spiritual Prayer 23
5: Method of Attaining to True Prayer ... 28
6: On Spiritual Dryness 37
7: On Defects and Infirmities 44
8: On Temptations and Tribulations 46
9: On Self-Denial 54
10: On Mortification 59
11: On Resignation 61
12: On Virtue 64
13: On Conversion 65
14: On Self-Annihilation 68
15: Man Acts More Nobly Under
   the Divine Influence, Than
   He Can Possibly Do by
   Following His Own Will 71
16: On the Possession of Peace
   and Rest Before God 81
17: On Perfection, or the Union
   of the Soul with God 85

Introduction

A *Guide to True Peace* was first published in 1813 by the Quaker Community in England. The first edition was very well received. Because of this a new edition was offered in 1815. This 1815 edition was "corrected and enlarged" by the original compilers. The 'correcting' consisted of changing the order of some of the chapters, in some cases making the English flow more smoothly, and in clarifying some views which in the 1813 edition were somewhat obscure. The 'enlarged' refers to additional passages, judiciously added, to, once again, clarify the message of the *Guide*.

The 1815 edition became the standard for all subsequent editions of the *Guide*. All future editions are based on this 1815 edition. For example, the order of the Chapters has remained the one found in the 1815 edition.

The compilers, two British Quakers, William Backhouse and James Janson, gleaned passages from the writings of three continental Quietists: Miguel Molinos, Madam Guyon, and Archbishop Fenelon. These three were the main actors in the movement known as 'Quietism'. All three of them were interrogated by the Inquisition for heresy. Molinos died in prison. Madam Guyon was imprisoned four times. Archbishop Fenelon was exiled from Paris and lived out his life in Cambray.

The result of these attacks was that Protestants felt free to borrow from these Catholic thinkers without themselves becoming too Catholic. The Quietists' writings had a surprisingly wide influence among the Pietists in Lutheran Germany, and among Protestants in England such as John Wesley.

The Quaker community in England also found the teachings of Quietism to be in sympathy with their own Faith and Practice. Quakers became a significant conduit for the spread of continental Quietism into Protestant lands. The culmination of this interest was the publication of the *Guide to True Peace*. The compilers of the *Guide* selected passages from the continental Quietists and wove them together into a seamless whole. In addition, the compilers also wove into the fabric copious biblical quotations; over 100 such biblical references are found in this work of roughly ninety pages. The result is a well-woven fabric that people have found of great value for 200 years. The *Guide* has been in continuous print and there are many editions available. Some of the currently available editions are from reprint houses and some are 'modernized' for today's audience. Editing of the modernized editions varies from having a light touch to substantial changes.

But I have noticed that this 1815 edition, the edition that all subsequent editions are derived from, is not currently available. On this two hundredth anniversary of the original publication of the *Guide* I have decided to make it once again accessible to a wide audience by using print-on-demand technology. This is a resetting of the 1815 Edition, published by W. Alexander, of York. The one change I have made is that in the 1815 Edition biblical references were footnoted at the bottom of the page. I have placed them in the body of the text, which is a procedure followed by many subsequent editions of the *Guide*. And I have decided to use the more familiar way of referencing biblical passages so that instead of "John i. 9.", I have used "John 1:9", and instead of "1 Cor. xii. 7.", I have used "1 Corinthians 12:7". In other words, I have dropped the use of roman numerals in biblical citations. In addition, I added a few biblical references which appear in later editions of the *Guide*, distinguishing these by placing them within distinctive brackets: { }. Otherwise, I have not changed the text.

In particular, I have not changed the spelling or modernized the language. The spelling, therefore, is that of British English. So, for example, you will find 'endeavour' instead of 'endeavor'. The English of the *Guide* is not difficult; countless readers have found it easy to comprehend for over 200 years. In my opinion, the *Guide* does not need any editing of its language. Nor does it need any editing of its style or paragraphing; something contemporary editors tend to do. There is a reason I feel this way: I find the *Guide* to be, on a literary level, a masterpiece of flowing prose. This is all the more surprising given the numerous sources used to put the *Guide* together. But it all works; there is a kind of current, or river-like pulse, to the *Guide* which is one of its greatest assets. I mean that the prose itself embodies the nature of the inward silence, the experience of the inward silence. The prose itself is a masterful teaching of the meaning of the prayer of inward silence.

My personal relationship to the *Guide* developed from my initial discovery of it after becoming a member of my local Quaker Meeting in 2010. I was exploring older Quaker works and some Quaker history. In the history I was reading the *Guide* was mentioned as a widely read and influential work among Quakers in the nineteenth and twentieth centuries. I found a used copy online; the Pendle Hill edition originally published in 1979 with the 'Introduction' by Howard Brinton. I immediately took to it. I have carried it with me ever since.

I then began exploring the history of the *Guide* and became aware that there have been numerous editions published since it first appeared in 1813. Each edition has made alterations. Most of these changes are minor; but some are significant. Eventually I discovered that all the variations can be traced back to changes in the 1815 edition of the *Guide*. I was finally able to track down a copy of the 1815 edition. It is a great privilege to be able to offer this edition once again to the general public.

In closing I want to note that I have done my best with the typing, uploading, and the other processes involved in getting this book to publication. Even so, there may be some mistakes that have slipped by me. If any reader finds such mistakes, or if any reader simply wants to discuss the *Guide* please feel free to contact me at:

Jim Wilson
P.O. Box 2756
Sebastopol, CA 95473

Acknowledgements:

Without the help of many people I would not have been able to follow through, and complete, this project. My Monthly Meeting has been greatly encouraging. Two friends of many years, Rob Schmidt and Stuart Goodnick consistently supported the time I spent on the *Guide*. Ruah Bull, my spiritual adviser, helped in more ways than she is aware of.

Finally, two librarians spent much time and effort tracking down early editions of the *Guide* for me. Tabitha Driver, the librarian of the London Yearly Meeting offered encouragements and assistance. And Ann Upton of the Haverford Quaker Collection tracked down early sources that I was unable to find elsewhere.

A Guide to True Peace

Preface

It was said by our blessed Redeemer that, "They who worship the Father, must worship Him in Spirit and in Truth." (John 4:24.) Now the object of this work is to explain, in a simple and familiar manner, how this only true worship can be acceptably performed, and inward, spiritual Prayer rightly attained. Few authors have written with greater clearness thereon, than those from whose works this little volume has been chiefly compiled; they, therefore, have been preferred: at the same time, it has been thought necessary to simplify, and render more intelligible, some of their terms, in order that they may be more generally understood.

Whilst some, into whose hands, this little treatise may fall, may receive it as a Messenger of glad Tidings, there will doubtless, be others, who may not feel disposed to place much dependance on the simple manner here pointed out, of drawing near to their Creator; let such, however, not judge according to the appearance; but, laying aside all reasoning thereon, in humility and simplicity make trial of it, and feel for themselves, whether, what is herein stated will not prove to be something more than an empty dream of the imagination, or a cunningly devised fable. And, if they do this in sincerity of heart, they will soon have to acknowledge, to their great consolation, that these are indeed substantial, efficacious, and incontrovertible Truths; and that this is the true way to become purified from our many defilements, to be instructed in heavenly mysteries, to taste of the wine of the kingdom, and to partake of that bread which nourisheth up unto everlasting life.

Chapter 1

The Spirit of God Dwells in the Heart of Man.

It is certain from Scripture that the Spirit of God dwells within us, that a "manifestation of this Spirit is given to us to profit withal," (1 Corinthians 12:7) and that this is "the true Light, which lighteth every man that cometh into the world." (John 1:9.) "This is the Grace of God, which bringeth Salvation, and which hath appeared unto all men; teaching us, that denying ungodliness and worldly lusts, we should live soberly, righteously, and godly, in this present world." (Titus 2:12.) But we make too little account of this internal Teacher, which is the soul of our soul, and by which only we are able to form good thoughts and desires. God ceases not to reprove us for evil, and to influence us to that which is good; but the noise of the world without and of our own passions within, deafen us, and hinder us from hearing Him.

We must retire from all outward objects, and silence all the desires and wandering imaginations of the mind that in this profound silence of the whole soul, we may hearken to the ineffable voice of the Divine Teacher. We must listen with an attentive ear, for it is a still, small voice. It is not indeed a voice uttered in words as when a man speaks to his friend; but it is a perception infused by the secret operations and influences of the Divine Spirit, insinuating to us obedience, patience, meekness, humility, and all the other Christian virtues, in a language perfectly intelligible to the attentive soul. But how seldom is it that the soul keeps itself silent enough for God to speak! The murmurs of our vain desires, and of our self-love, disturb all the teachings of the Divine Spirit. Ought we then to be surprised, if so many persons, apparently devout, but too full of their own wisdom, and confidence in their own virtues, are not able to hear it; and that they look upon this internal Word as the chimera of fanatics? Alas! what is it they aim at with their vain reasoning? The external word, even of the Gospel, would be but an empty sound without this living and fruitful Word in the interior, to interpret and open it to the understanding.

Jesus Christ saith: "Behold, I stand at the door, and knock – if any man hear my voice, and open the door, I will come unto him, and sup with him, and he with me." (Revelation 3:20.) His knocks are the monitions of His Spirit; which touches us, and operates in us.

And to attend to these monitions and follow them, is to open unto Him.

God speaks in impenitent sinners; but these, engrossed in the eager pursuit of worldly pleasures, and the gratification of their evil passions, are not able to hear Him. His word with them passes for a fable. But wo unto those who receive their consolation in this life. The time will come when their vain joys shall be confounded.

He speaks in sinners who are in the way of conversion: these feel the remorses of their conscience, and these remorses are the voice of God, which upbraids them inwardly with their vices. When they are truly touched they have no difficulty to comprehend this secret voice, for it is this that so pierces them to the quick. It is that two-edged sword within them, of which St. Paul speaks, which goes even to the dividing of the soul from itself: "The word of God is quick and powerful, and sharper than any two-edged sword; piercing even to the dividing asunder of soul and spirit, and of the joints and marrow; and is a discerner of the thoughts and intents of the heart." (Hebrews 4:12.)

He speaks in persons enlightened, learned, and whose life, exteriorly regular, seems adorned with many virtues; but often these persons, full of themselves, and of their knowledge, give too much ear to themselves to listen to God. God, who seeks only to communicate himself, finds no place (so to speak) where to introduce himself into these souls, that are so full of themselves, and so overfed with their own wisdom and virtues. He hides His secrets from the wise and prudent, and reveals them to the low and simple: our blessed Redeemer said: "I thank thee, Oh Father, Lord of heaven and earth! because thou hast hid these things from the wise and prudent, and hast revealed them unto babes." (Matthew 11:25.) It is with the humble and child-like that He delights to dwell, and to disclose to them his ineffable secrets. It is these who are more peculiarly qualified for receiving in a greater measure the gift of faith; for, being willing that the pride of Reason should be laid in the dust, they obstruct not the entrance of this gift by their vain arguments; but believe with simplicity and confidence.

Chapter 2

On Faith

There are two sorts or degrees of Faith: - the first is, that by which the mind gives its assent to the truth of a thing on the testimony of another; the second is of a more exalted nature, being of Divine origin, and is a gift of the Holy Spirit. By the first, we believe in the existence of God, and in the truths which He has revealed to us in the Holy Scriptures. It is an essential principle in the beginning of the spiritual path; for "he that cometh to God, must believe that He is God, and that He is a rewarder of them that diligently seek Him." (Hebrews 11:6.) And if we put our whole trust in Him, and endeavour in all things to obey Him, we shall be in a state of preparation for the reception of that true and living Faith which is "the gift of God." (Ephesians 2:8.)

It is only by this Faith that we shall be enabled to overcome all our spiritual enemies, and clearly to understand those mysteries which are incomprehensible to human reason; for reason being born of man, is weak and uncertain, and easily errs; but faith, being born of God, cannot err; reason, therefore, must follow and submit to faith, not go before and control it.

It is by Faith that, "being justified, we have peace with God, through our Lord Jesus Christ." (Romans 5:1.) And when this precious gift has been granted to us, it produces in us Hope (Romans 5:2), Love (1 Peter 1:8), Confidence (Ephesians 3:12), Joy (Romans 5:2), and Holiness (Acts 15:9) of heart. We shall then be enabled to feel an entire dependance on the goodness, power, justice, and mercy of God, and a confidence in His promises; as well as more fully to experience and comprehend the operations of His Spirit on the mind.

Faith is an essential requisite for the proper performance of all our duties to God: indeed, without it we cannot possibly please Him (Hebrews 11:6); neither should we ever be induced to seek Him, or believe in the influence of His Holy Spirit upon our Souls. It is by Faith that we are supported in our path to Peace, and are enabled to persevere through the difficulties and besetments, which we may have to encounter on our way: it is through this holy principle that we suffer the pains of dryness, and want of consolation, without fainting; being thereby strengthened to "endure, as seeing Him who is invisible." (Hebrews 11:27.) And it is only by Faith that we can attain to the practice of true, inward, and spiritual prayer.

Chapter 3

On Prayer

Prayer is an intercourse of the soul with God.*   It is not a work of the head, but of the heart; which ought always to continue. It is the medium through which life and food are conveyed to the soul, and the channel through which the gifts and graces of the Holy Spirit flow and are communicated. Every secret aspiration of the soul to God is prayer: all are therefore capable of prayer, and are called thereto, as all are called to, and are capable of, Salvation.

St. Paul hath enjoined us to "pray without ceasing" (1 Thessalonians 5:17); and our Lord saith: "I say unto all, watch and pray." (Mark 13:33, 37 and 14:38.) Come, then, all ye that are athirst, to these living waters (Revelation 22:17){John 7:37}; nor lose our precious moments in "hewing out cisterns that will hold no water." (Jeremiah 2:13.) Come, ye famishing souls who find nought whereon to feed; come, and ye shall be fully satisfied. Come, ye poor afflicted ones, who groan beneath your load of wretchedness and pain, and ye shall find ease and comfort. Come, ye sick, to your Physician, and be not fearful of approaching Him, because you are filled with diseases; expose them to His view, and they shall be healed.

Children, draw near to your Father, and he will embrace you in the arms of Love. Come, ye poor, stray, wandering sheep, return to your Shepherd. Come ye who have been seeking happiness in worldly pleasures and pursuits; but have failed to find in them that satisfaction ye expected: come, and learn how to be truly happy here, and eternally happy hereafter. Come, sinners, to your Saviour. Come, ye dull, ignorant, and illiterate; ye who think yourselves the most incapable of prayer: ye are more peculiarly called, and adapted thereto. Let all, without exception, come; for Jesus Christ hath called all.

You must however learn a species of prayer which may be exercised at all times, which doth not obstruct outward employments, and which may be equally practised by all ranks and conditions of men; by the poor as well as the rich, by the illiterate as well as the learned. It cannot, therefore, be a prayer of the head, but of the heart. It is a species of prayer which nothing can interrupt but irregular and disordered affections. And though you may think yourselves ever so dull, and incapable of sublime attainments, yet, by prayer, the possession and enjoyment of God is easily obtained; for He is more desirous to give Himself to us than we can be to receive Him.

Prayer is the guide to perfection, and the sovereign good; it delivers us from every vice, and obtains for us every virtue: for the one great means to become perfect, is to walk in the presence of God. He himself has said: Walk in my presence, and be thou perfect. (Genesis 17:1). It is only by prayer that we are brought into, and maintained in, His presence; and when once we have fully known Him, and the sweetness of His love, we shall find it impossible to relish any thing so much as Himself.

===

*God is a Spirit; so is the mind. Bodies can have intercourse; so can souls. When minds are in an assimilating state of purity, they have union with their Maker. This was the bliss of paradise: sin interrupted, and holiness must restore it. To a soul thus distressed, the Creator communicates Himself, in a manner which is as insensible to the natural eye, as the falling of dew; but not less refreshing in its secret powers, than the dew is to vegetation.

Anonymous Essay on Devotion

Chapter 4

All are Capable of Attaining to Inward, and Spiritual Prayer

If all were solicitous to pursue the spiritual path, shepherds, while they watched their flocks, might have the Spirit of the primitive Christians, and the husbandman at the plough, maintain a blessed intercourse with his God; the manufacturer, while he exhausted his outward man with labour, would be renewed in internal strength: every species of vice would shortly disappear, and all mankind become true followers of the Good Shepherd.

Oh when once the heart is gained, how easily is all moral evil corrected! It is, for this reason, that God, above all things, requires the heart. It is the conquest of the heart alone, that can extirpate these dreadful vices which are so predominant amongst men; such as drunkenness, blasphemy, lewdness, envy, and theft. Jesus Christ would become the universal and peaceful Sovereign, and the hearts of all mankind would be wholly renewed.

The decay of internal piety, is unquestionably the source of the various errors that have arisen in the world; all of which would speedily be sapped and overthrown, were inward religion to be established. If, instead of engaging our wandering brethren in vain disputes, we could but teach them simply to believe, and diligently to pray, we should lead them sweetly unto God.

Oh how inexpressibly great is the loss sustained by mankind, from the neglect of the interior!

Some excuse themselves by saying that this is a dangerous way; pleading the incapacity of simple persons to comprehend spiritual matters. But the Oracles of Truth affirm the contrary. Isaiah saith: "The way-faring men, though fools, shall not err therein." (Isaiah 35:8.) And where can be the danger of walking in the only true way (John 14:6), which is Jesus Christ? of giving ourselves to Him, fixing our eye continually on Him, placing all our confidence in His grace, and turning with all the strength of our soul to His pure love?

The simple, so far from being incapable of this perfection, are by their docility, innocency, and humility, peculiarly adapted and qualified for its attainment; and as they are not accustomed to reasoning, they are less employed in speculations, less tenacious of their own opinions. Even from their want of learning, they submit more freely to the teachings of the Divine Spirit; whereas others, who are blinded by self-sufficiency, and enslaved by prejudice, give great resistance to the operations of Grace.

We are told in Scripture, "that unto the simple, God giveth understanding" (Psalm 119:130); and we are also assured, that God careth for them: "The Lord preserveth the simple." (Psalm 116:6.) Christ said to his Apostles; "Suffer little children to come unto me, for of such is the kingdom of Heaven." (Matthew 19:14.)

The simple are incapable of reasoning, teach them, therefore, the prayer of the heart, not of the head; the prayer of God's Spirit, not of man's invention.

Alas! by wanting them to pray in elaborate forms, and to be curiously critical therein, you create their chief obstacles. The children have been led astray from the best of Fathers, by your endeavouring to teach them too refined, too polished a language.

The simple and undisguised emotions of filial love are infinitely more expressive than the most studied language. The Spirit of God needs none of our arrangements and methods:

when it pleaseth Him, he turns Shepherds into Prophets; and, so far from excluding any from the Temple of Prayer, He throws wide open the gates, that all may enter in; while "Wisdom crieth, Whoso is simple let him turn in hither; as for him that wanteth understanding, she saith to him, Come, eat of my bread, and drink of the wine which I have mingled." (Proverbs 9:3, 4, 5.)

To teach man to seek God in his heart, to think of Him, to return to Him whenever he has wandered from Him, and to do and suffer all things with a single eye to please Him, is the natural and ready process; it is leading the soul to the very source of Grace, wherein is to be found all that is necessary for sanctification.

Oh that all would at once put themselves into this way, which is Jesus Christ, that His Kingdom might be established in their hearts! For as it is the heart alone that can oppose His sovereignty, it is by the subjection of the heart that His sovereignty is most highly exalted. And since none can attain this blessed state, save those whom God Himself leads and places therein; we do not pretend to introduce any into it, but only to point out the shortest and safest road that leads to it: beseeching you not to be retarded in your progress by any external exercises; not to rest in the shadow, instead of the substance. If the water of eternal life is shown to some thirsty souls, how inexpressibly cruel would it be, by confining them to a round of external forms, to prevent their approaching it: so that their longing shall never be satisfied, but they shall perish with thirst!

Oh ye blind and foolish men, who pride yourselves on science, wisdom, wit, and power! How well do you verify what God hath said, that His secrets are hidden from the wise and prudent, and revealed unto *The Little Ones – The Babes.* {Matthew 11:25.}

Chapter 5

Method of Attaining to True Prayer

The sort of prayer to which we have alluded, is that of inward silence; wherein the soul, abstracted from all outward things, in holy stillness, humble reverence, and lively faith, waits patiently to feel the Divine Presence, and to receive the precious influences of the Holy Spirit. And when you retire for this purpose, which should be your frequent practice, you should consider yourself as being placed in the presence of God, looking with a single eye to Him, resigning yourself entirely into His hands, to receive from Him whatsoever He may be pleased to dispense to you; calmly endeavouring, at the same time, to fix your mind in peace and silence; quitting all your own reasonings, and not willingly thinking on any thing, how good, and how profitable soever it may appear to be. And should any vain imaginations present themselves, you should gently turn from them; and thus faithfully and patiently wait to feel the Divine Presence.

If, while you are thus engaged, something of inward stillness, or a degree of the softening influence of the Divine Spirit, is mercifully granted you, you should prize these manifestations of the Presence of God in your soul, and be carefully, and reverently, attentive thereto; being cautious, however, not to endeavour to increase them by your own activity; for, by so doing, you will draw the mind off from that state of holy stillness, and humble watchfulness, which you should be solicitous as much as possible to maintain: by fanning the flame there is a danger of extinguishing it, and thus depriving the soul of that nourishment which was intended for it.

A lively sense of the Presence of God, will extricate us speedily from numberless mental wanderings, remove us far from external objects, and bring us nigh unto our God, who is only to be found in our inmost centre; which is the Temple where he dwelleth. (1 Corinthians 3:16.) And when we are thus fully turned inward and warmly penetrated with a sense of His Presence, we should in stillness and repose, with reverence, confidence, and love, suffer the blessed food of which we have tasted, to sink deep into the soul.

The prayer of inward silence is the easiest and most profitable path, because that with a simple view, or attention to God, the soul becomes like a humble supplicant before its Lord; or as a child that casts itself into the safe bosom of its mother. It is also the most secure, because it is abstracted from the operations of the imagination; which being always exposed to the delusions of the enemy, is often beguiled into extravagancies, and is easily bewildered and deceived; the soul being thereby deprived of its peace.

It will at first be difficult, from the habit the mind will have acquired of being always from home, roving hither and thither, and from subject to subject, to restrain it, and free it from these wanderings which are an impediment to prayer. -- Indeed those wanderings of the imagination with which beginners are for some time tried, are permitted in order to prove their faith, exercise their patience, and to show them how little they can perform of themselves; as well as to teach them to depend upon God alone for strength to overcome all their difficulties; "for by" his own "strength, shall no man prevail" (1 Samuel 2:9); and if they place all their hope in Him, and faithfully persevere, every obstacle will be gradually removed, and they will find that they will be enabled to approach Him with facility, and that inward silence is not only attended with much less difficulty, but at times will be found to be easy, sweet, and delightful. They will know that this is the true way of finding God; and feel "His name to be an ointment poured forth." (Canticles 1:3.)

And although we should at all times be very watchful and diligent in recalling our wandering thoughts, restraining them, as much as may be, in due subjection; yet a direct contest with them only serves to augment and irritate them; whereas, by calling to mind that we are in the presence of God, and endeavouring to sink down under a sense and perception thereof, simply turning inwards; we wage insensibly a very advantageous, though indirect, war with them.

Those who have not learned to read are not, on that account, excluded from prayer; for the great Teacher who teacheth all things, is Jesus Christ himself. (John 14:26.) They should learn this fundamental rule, that "the Kingdom of God is within them" (Luke 17:21); and that it is there only it must be sought.

"The Kingdom of God is within you," saith our blessed Redeemer. Abandon, therefore, the cares and pleasures of this wretched world, and turn to the Lord with all your heart, and your soul shall find rest. (Matthew 11:28, 29.) If you withdraw your attention from outward things, and keep it fixed on the internal Teacher, endeavouring to obey Him in whatsoever He may require of you, you will soon perceive the coming of the kingdom of God (Matthew 6:10): for the kingdom of God is that "peace and joy in the Holy Ghost" (Romans 14:17), which cannot be received by sensual and worldly men.

It is for want of inward retirement, and prayer, that our lives are so imperfect, and that we are neither penetrated nor warmed with the divine Light of Truth, Christ the Light. (John 1:9.) We should, therefore, be in the daily practice of it; and there are none so much occupied, as not to be able to find a few moments of inward retirement to God. The less we practise silent prayer, the less desire we have for it; for our minds being set upon outward things, we contract at last such a habit, that it is very hard to turn them inward.

"The Lord is in His Holy Temple, let all the earth keep silence before Him." (Habakkuk 2:20.) The silence of all our earthly thoughts and desires is absolutely indispensible, if we would hear the secret voice of the Divine Instructer. Hearing is a sense formed to receive sounds, and is rather passive than active, admitting but not communicating sensation; and if we would hear, we must lend the ear for that purpose; so, Christ, The Eternal Word (Revelation 19:13), without whose

Divine inspeaking the soul is dead, dark, and barren, when He would speak within us, requires the most silent attention to His all-quickening and efficacious voice.

We should forget ourselves, and all self-interest, and listen and be attentive to the voice of our God. Outward silence is very requisite for the cultivation and improvement of inward; and, indeed, it is impossible we should become truly internal, without the love and practice of outward silence and retirement. And unquestionably our being internally engaged with God, is wholly incompatible with being busied, and employed in the numerous trifles that surround us.

When through inadvertency or unfaithfulness we become dissipated, or as it were uncentred, it is of immediate importance to turn again gently and peacefully inward; and thus we may learn to preserve the spirit and unction of prayer, throughout the day: for if the prayer of inward silence were wholly confined to any appointed half-hour, or hour, we should reap but little fruit.

It is of the greatest importance, for the soul to go to prayer with confidence; and such a pure and disinterested love, as seeks nothing from God, but the ability to please Him, and to do His Will; for a servant who only proportions his diligence to his hope of reward, renders himself unworthy of all reward. Go, then, to prayer, not that ye may enjoy spiritual delights, but that ye may be full or empty, just as it pleaseth God. This will preserve you in an evenness of spirit, either in desertion or in consolation, and will prevent your being surprised at dryness, or the apparent repulses of God.

Constant prayer is, to keep the heart always right towards God. Strive then, when you come from prayer, not to suffer your mind to be too much entangled with outward things, endeavouring to be totally resigned to the Divine Will; that God may do with you and yours according to His heavenly pleasure, relying on Him as on a kind and loving Father; and though you be taken up with your outward affairs, and your mind thereby prevented from being actually fixed on Him, even then, you will always carry a fire about you that will never go out; but which, on the contrary, will nourish a secret prayer, that will be like a lamp continually lighted before the throne of God.

A son who loves his Father does not always think distinctly of him; many objects draw away his mind, but these never interrupt the filial love; whenever his Father returns into his thoughts, he loves him, and he feels, in the very inmost of his heart, that he has never discontinued one moment to love him, though he has ceased to think of him. In this manner should we love our heavenly Father. It is by Religion alone that we are enabled to call God, Father, and that we can indeed become His sons.

True Religion is a heaven-born thing, it is an emanation of the Truth and Goodness of God upon the spirits of men, whereby they are formed into a similitude and likeness of Himself, and become "partakers of the Divine Nature." (2 Peter 1:4.) A true Christian is every way of a most noble extraction, of a heavenly and divine pedigree, being born, as St. John expresseth it, "from above." (John 3:3 – See marginal reading.) And in another place he saith; "Behold what manner of love the Father hath bestowed upon us, that we should be called the sons of God!" (1 John 3:1.)

If considerations such as these, are not sufficient to convince us of the folly of our attachment to perishing things, and to stimulate us to press after those which obtain for us such great and glorious privileges, we must, indeed, be sunk into a state of deep and deplorable insensibility; out of which, even "if one were to rise from the dead" (Luke 16:31.) for that purpose, it would be impossible to arouse us.

Note: If you wish to receive real profit from the Holy Scriptures and other spiritual books, you must peruse them with deep attention, and introversion of mind, observing, whatever you have chosen, to read only a small part of it; endeavouring to taste and digest it, to extract the essence and substance thereof; and proceed no further, while any savour or relish remains in the passage: when this subsides, take up your book again, and proceed as before, seldom reading more than half a page at a time; for it is not the quantity that is read, but the manner of reading, that yields us profit. Those who read fast, reap no more advantage than a bee would do by only skimming over the surface of a flower, instead of waiting to penetrate into it, and extract its sweets. If this method were persued, we should be more fully disposed for retirement and prayer.

Guyon

Chapter 6

On Spiritual Dryness

No sooner will you have given yourself up to serve the Lord in this inward way, than he will begin to purify you, and try your Faith; in order to draw you nearer to Himself. And, for this purpose, He will lead you through the paths of dryness and desertion; so that, when you endeavour to fix your mind in silence, in order to feel after your God, you will not experience the comfort and refreshment you expected; but, on the contrary, you will be more than usually beset with a multitude of troublesome and importunate imaginations; insomuch, that you will begin to think that you labour to no purpose, and that the prayer of internal silence is an attainment to which you need not aspire, seeing that your imagination is so ungovernable, and your mind so void of good. But this state of dryness is very profitable, if it be suffered with patience.

The Lord makes use of the veil of dryness, to the end we may not know what he is working in us, and so may be humble; because, if we felt, and knew, what he was working in our souls, satisfaction and presumption would get in; we should imagine we were doing some good thing, and reckon ourselves very near to God; and this self-complacency would prevent our spiritual advancement.

And, though in the prayer of mental stillness, you may feel yourself to be in a dry and comfortless state, not being able to get rid of your troublesome thoughts, nor experience any light, consolation, or spiritual feeling, yet be not afflicted, nor desist from your undertaking; resign yourself at that time with vigour, and patiently persevere as in His presence; for, while you persevere in that manner, your soul will be internally improved.

Do you believe, that when you come from prayer in the same manner as you begun it, without feeling yourself profited thereby, that you have been toiling in vain. That is a fallacy; because true prayer consists, not in enjoying the light, and having knowledge of spiritual things, but in enduring with patience, and persevering in faith and silence; believing that you are in the Lord's presence, turning to Him your heart with tranquillity and simplicity of mind.

We must be aware that nature is always an enemy to the spirit; and, that, when she is deprived of sensible pleasures, she remains weak, melancholy, and full of irksomeness.

Hence from the uneasiness of thoughts, the lassitude of body, importunate sleep, and your inability to curb the senses, every one of which would follow its own pleasure; you will often feel impatient to be at the end of your prayer. Happy are you if you can persevere amidst this painful trial! Remember, that "They who wait upon the Lord shall renew their strength; they shall mount up with wings as eagles; they shall run and not be weary, they shall walk and not faint." (Isaiah 40:31.)

The prayer of internal silence may be well typified by that wrestling, which the Holy Scriptures say, the patriarch Jacob had all night with God, until the day broke, and He blessed him. Wherefore, the soul is to persevere, and wrestle with the difficulties that it will meet with in inward prayer, without desisting, until the Sun of internal Light begin to appear, and the Lord give it His blessing.

If you go to prayer with the spirit and intention of praying, so long as you retract not that intention, although, through misery and frailty, your thoughts may wander, you will, nevertheless, pray in spirit and in truth. God, in his own due time, will help you to overcome all your difficulties; and, when least you think, will give you holy purposes, and more effectual desires of serving Him. Distrust not

Him, therefore, but only yourself; and remember that, as the apostle saith, "He is the Father of mercies, and God of all comforts." (2 Corinthians 1:3.) His comforts are sometimes withdrawn, but His mercy endureth for ever. He hath deprived you of what was sweet and sensible in His grace, because you required to be humbled.

Be of good courage then, and though it may seem to you that you toil without gaining much advantage, yet you must recollect, we must plough and sow before we can reap; and if you persevere in faith and patience, you will reap an abundant reward for all your labours. Would you be so unreasonable, as to expect to find without seeking; or for it to be opened to you, without your taking the pains to knock? As well might the husbandman expect to see his fields waving with grain, without his having been at the trouble to put the seed into the ground.

It is no hard matter to adhere to God, while you are in the enjoyment of his comforts and consolations; but if you would prove your fidelity to Him, you must be willing to follow Him through the paths of dryness and desertion. The truth of a friend is not known, while he is receiving favours and benefits from us; but if he remain faithful to us when we treat him with coldness and neglect, it will be a proof of the sincerity of his attachment.

Though God hath no other desire, than to impart Himself to those that love and seek Him; yet He frequently conceals Himself from us, that we may be roused from sloth, and induced to seek Him with fidelity and love. But, with what abundant goodness doth he recompense our faithfulness! and how sweetly are these apparent withdrawings of Himself succeeded by the consolations of His Love! David saith, "I waited patiently for the Lord; and He inclined unto me, and heard my cry. He brought me up also out of a horrible pit, out of the miry clay, and set my feet upon a rock, and established my goings. And he hath put a new song in my mouth; even praise unto our God." (Psalm 40:1, 2, 3.)

In seasons of the withdrawings of His Presence, we are apt to believe that it will be a proof of our fidelity, and evince the ardour of our love, to seek Him by an exertion of our *own* strength and activity; and that this exertion will induce Him the more speedily to return. But this is not the right procedure, when we are in this state; with patient resignation, with self-abasement, with the reiterated breathings of an ardent, but peaceful affection, and with reverential silence, we must wait the return of our beloved. Thus, only, we shall demonstrate, that we seek nothing but Himself, and his good pleasure; and not the selfish delights of our own sensations.

It is very common for us, when we feel the sweetness of the grace of God, to fancy that we love Him; but it is only in the withdrawings of His Presence that our love can be tried, and the measure of it known. It is at these seasons that we are convinced of the weakness and misery of our nature, and how incapable we are, of ourselves, to think or do any good. There are many who, when they experience meltings of heart, shedding of tears, and other sensible delights, imagine that they are favourites of God, and that then they truly possess Him; and so pass all their lives in seeking after those pleasurable sensations; but they should be cautious lest they deceive themselves; for these consolations, when they proceed from nature and are occasioned by their own reflections, or self-admirings, hinder them from discerning the true light, or making one step towards perfection. You should therefore be attentive to distinguish those meltings of the affections, from the operations which purely proceed from God, leaving yourselves to be led forward by Him; who will be your light in the midst of darkness and dryness.

It is of no small advantage in prayer, patiently to suffer the want of consolation, and the trouble and importunities of a wandering imagination; it is an offering up of one's self in a whole burnt offering and sacrifice. And as many times as you exercise yourself, calmly to reject your vain thoughts, and, peacefully to endure your dark and desolate state, so many crowns will the Lord set upon your head.

It is of great importance that you endeavour, at all times, to keep your heart in peace; that you may keep pure that temple of God. The way to keep it in peace, is, to enter into it by means of inward silence. When you see yourself more sharply assaulted, retreat into that region of peace; and you will find a fortress that will enable you to triumph over all your enemies, visible and invisible, and over all their snares and temptations. Within your own soul resides Divine Aid, and Sovereign Succour. Retreat within it, and all will be quiet, secure, peaceable, and calm. Thus, by means of mental silence, which can only be attained by Divine Help, you may look for tranquillity in tumult; solitude in company; light in darkness; forgetfulness in pressures; vigour in despondency; courage in fear; resistance in temptation; peace in war; and quiet in tribulation.

Chapter 7

On Defects and Infirmities

Should we so far get off our guard, as again to wander among externals in search of happiness, or sink into dissipation, or commit a fault, we must instantly turn inwards; for having departed thereby from our God, we should as soon as possible return unto Him, and patiently suffer whatever sensations he is pleased to impress: for He has declared, "as many as I love I rebuke and chasten." (Revelation 3:19.)

On the commission of a fault, it is of great importance to guard against vexation and disquietude, which spring from a secret root of pride, and a love of our own excellence; we are hurt by feeling what we are: and if we discourage ourselves, or despond, we are the more enfeebled; and from our reflections on the fault a chagrin arises, which is often worse than the fault itself.

The truly humble soul is not surprised at its defects or failings; and the more miserable and wretched it beholds itself, the more doth it abandon itself unto God, and press for a nearer and more intimate alliance with Him, that it may avail itself of an eternal strength. We should the rather be induced to act thus, as God Himself hath said: "I will instruct thee and teach thee in the way which thou shalt go: I will guide thee with mine eye." (Psalm 32:8.)

Chapter 8

On Temptations and Tribulations

We are by nature so base, proud, and ambitious; and so full of our own appetites, our own judgment and opinions, that if temptations and tribulations were not permitted to try, humble, and purify us, we should never arrive at a state of acceptance with God.

The Lord, seeing our misery, and perverse inclinations, and being thereby moved to compassion, withdraws his strength from us, that we may feel our own weakness; suffering us to be assaulted by violent and painful suggestions of impatience and pride, and divers other temptations: and some, who have long been in the practice of sin, by gluttony, luxury, rage, swearing, despair, and a great many other besetments; in order that they may know themselves, and be humble. With these temptations, Infinite Goodness humbles our pride; giving us, in them, the most wholesome medicine.

"All our righteousness," as Isaiah saith, "are as filthy rags" (Isaiah 64:6); through the vanity, conceitedness, and self-love, with which they are defiled. It is, therefore, necessary that they should be purified with the fire of temptation and tribulation; that so they may be clean, pure, perfect, and acceptable in the sight of God. {James 1:2-4.}

The Lord polishes the soul which he draws to himself, with the rough file of temptation; freeing it thereby, from the rust of many evil passions and propensities. By means of temptation and tribulation He humbles, subjects, and exercises it; showing it its own weakness and misery. It is thus that He purifies and strips the heart; in order that all its operations may be pure, and of inestimable value. Oh, how happy would you be, if you could quietly believe, that all the trials and temptations wherewith you are assaulted, are permitted for your gain and spiritual profit!

But you will perhaps say, that when you are molested by others, or wronged and injured by your neighbour, that this cannot be for your spiritual advantage; seeing, that it is the effect of their faults and malice. This is no other than a cunning and hidden device of the enemy; because, though God wills not the sin of another, yet He wills His own effects in you; and the trouble which accrues to you from another's fault should improve you by increasing your patience and exercising your forbearance and charity.

Consider, how the Lord makes use of the faults of others for the good of your soul. Oh, the greatness of the divine wisdom! who can pry into the depth of the secret and extraordinary means, and the hidden ways, whereby He guides the soul which he desires to purge, transform, and dignify.

It is often the greatest temptation to be without temptation; because we are then most liable to fall into a state of lukewarmness; wherefore, we ought not to repine when it assaults us; but with resignation, peace, and constancy, shut our hearts against it. If you would serve God, and arrive at the sublime region of internal peace, you must pass through this rugged path of temptation and tribulation; and therein become polished, purged, renewed, and purified.

A direct contest and struggle with temptations rather serves to augment them; and withdraws the soul from that adherence to God, which it should ever be its principal occupation to strive after and maintain. The surest and safest method of conquest, is simply to turn away from the evil, and draw yet nearer and closer to our God: a little child, on perceiving a monster, does not wait to fight with it, and will scarcely turn its eyes towards it; but quickly shrinks into the bosom of its mother, in total confidence of safety; so, likewise, should the soul turn from the dangers of temptation to its God. "God is in the midst of her," saith the Psalmist, "she should not be moved; God shall help her, and that right early." (Psalm 46:5.) "The name of the Lord is a strong Tower to which the righteous flee and are safe." (Proverbs 18:10.)

If we do otherwise, and in our weakness attempt to attack our enemies, we shall frequently feel ourselves wounded, if not totally defeated: but, by casting ourselves into the presence of God, and relying solely on Him, we shall find supplies of strength for our support. This was the succour sought for by David: "I have set," saith he, "the Lord always before me: because he is at my right hand, I shall not be moved. Therefore, my heart is glad, and my glory rejoiceth: my flesh, also shall rest in hope." (Psalm 16:8, 9.) And, it is said in Exodus, "The Lord shall fight for you, and ye shall hold your peace." (Exodus 14:14.)

Although "God cannot be tempted with evil, neither tempteth He any man" (James 1:13); yet it is evident that temptations are permitted for our good, and, rightly endured, tend to our refinement; "therefore count it all joy, when ye fall into divers temptations; knowing this, that the trying of your faith worketh patience." (James 1:2.) And in all our besetments, however painful they may feel to us, or of whatever nature they may be, we should remember that it is said: "Blessed is the man that endureth temptation: for when he is tried, he shall receive the crown of life, which the Lord hath promised to them that love him." (James 1:12.)

You cannot be hurt by men or devils, if you keep always near to God; for, "who is he that will harm you, if ye be followers of that which is good." (1 Peter 3:13.) But if you are hurt, it is your pride, your passions, and your many unsubdued evil propensities, that rise up and injure you; and as long as these remain, the enemy will make use of them, and seek to draw your mind away from its adherence to God.

"Every man is tempted, when he is drawn away of his own lust, and enticed." (James 1:14.) Therefore know your own corrupt state, and the need you have to be purified by means of temptation, and keep always on the watch, lest the unwearied enemy gain access to your soul by his insinuations and pleasing allurements, which he will suit to your present situation and condition: for, in your passage through life, there are many things which he will offer you as temptations; endeavouring to produce in you an inordinate inclination and desire for them; which if you give way to whilst you are in this manner tempted, great will be the danger of your being wholly overcome.

If the malignant enemy is not resisted in his first attack, he enters by gradual advances, and takes entire possession of the heart; and so long as opposition is deferred by habitual negligence, the power of opposing becomes every day less, and the strength of the adversary proportionably greater. Therefore, when you feel in yourself a strong and eager desire after any thing whatsoever, and find your inclination carry you too precipitately to do it, strive to moderate yourself by retreating inwards, and seeking after tranquillity of mind. To do all things well, we must do them as in the presence of God, otherwise we shall soon get off our right centre, and be in danger of being wholly overthrown.

Oh, blessed soul! if you would but be content and quiet in the fire of temptation and tribulation, and suffer yourself to be fully proved and tried, in patiently enduring the assaults of the enemy and the desertion of heavenly good, how soon would you find yourself rich in celestial treasures! how soon would the Divine bounty make a rich throne in your soul, and a goodly habitation for you to refresh and solace yourself in! Know, that although the Lord may for a season *visit*, yet he taketh up His *abode* in none but peaceful souls; and those in whom the fire of temptation and tribulation hath consumed *all* their corrupt propensities: the Lord reposeth not Himself any where, but where quietness reigns, and self-love is banished.

If, from chaos, His Omnipotence has produced so many wonders in the creation of the world, what will He not do in your soul, created after His own image and likeness, if you keep constant, quiet, and resigned; with a true sense of your own nothingness?

"Cast not, therefore, away your confidence, which hath great recompense of reward" (Hebrews 10:35), but keep constant; O blessed soul! keep constant; for it will not be as you imagine: nor are you at any time nearer to God, than in such times of desertion, and trial of your faith; for, although the sun is hid in the clouds, yet it changes not its place, nor lose any part of its brightness. The Lord permits these painful temptations and desertions, to purge and polish you, to cleanse and disrobe you of self; that you may become by these trials entirely His, and give yourself up wholly to serve Him.

Oh how much is there to be purified in a soul, that must arrive at the holy mountain of perfection, and of transformation, with God! For, whilst any portion of evil, any thing of self, remains in us, we must be subject to temptation. When self is annihilated, there is then nothing left for the tempter to act upon. Oh, how resigned, naked, denied, annihilated, ought the soul to be, that would not hinder the entrance of the Divine Lord, nor his continual communion with it!

Chapter 9

On Self-Denial

He who expects to arrive at perfection, or a union of the soul with God, by means of consolation and comfort, will find himself mistaken. For, from the depravity of our nature, we must expect to suffer, and be in some measure purified, before we can be in any degree fitted for a union with God, or permitted to taste the joy of His Presence.

Be ye patient, therefore, under all the sufferings which God is pleased to send you. If your love to Him be pure, you will not seek him less in suffering than in consolation; and, surely, he should be as much loved in *that* as in *this*, since it was by suffering on the cross that He made the greater display of His own love for you.

Be not like those, who give themselves to Him at one season, and withdraw from Him at another. They give themselves only to be caressed; and wrest themselves back again, when they come to be crucified; or at least turn to the world for consolation.

No, ye will not find consolation in aught, but a free and full surrender of your will to the Divine Will. Who savoureth not the Cross, savoureth not the things that be of God (Matthew 16:23); and a heart that savoureth the Cross, finds the bitterest things to be sweet: "to the hungry soul every bitter thing is sweet." (Proverbs 27:7.) God giveth the Cross, and the Cross giveth us God.

We may be assured, that there is an internal advancement, where there is an advancement in the way of the Cross.

As soon as any thing presents itself as a suffering, and you feel a repugnance against it, resign yourself immediately unto God with respect to it, giving yourself up to Him in sacrifice; and you will find, that, when the Cross arrives, it will not be so very burdensome, because you had disposed yourself to a willing reception of it. Jesus Christ Himself was willing to suffer its utmost rigours. We often bear the cross in weakness, at other times in strength; all should be equal to us in the will of God.

If any other way, but bearing the cross, and dying to his own will, could have redeemed man from that fallen and corrupt state, in which he is by nature, Christ would have taught it by His example. But of all that desire to follow him, He has required the bearing of the cross; and without exception has said to all: "If any man will come after me, let him deny himself, take up his cross and follow me." (Matthew 16:24.) Why then do you fear to take up the cross, which will direct you to the path which leads to the kingdom of God?

From the cross are derived heavenly meekness, true fortitude, the joys of the spirit, the conquest of self, the perfection of holiness! There is no redemption, no hope of the continuation of the divine life in us, but by our taking up the cross to our carnal appetites, and inclinations: for all consists in the death of self, and there is no means to obtain life and peace, but by thus dying to the corruptions of our fallen nature! Take up your cross therefore, and follow Jesus, in the path that leads to everlasting peace. He hath gone before, bearing that cross upon which He died for you; that you might follow, patiently bearing your own, and, upon that, dying to yourself for Him. And if we die with Him, we shall also live with Him: "if we are partakers of His sufferings, we shall also be partakers of His glory." {Romans 8:17, 2 Corinthians 1:7, 2 Timothy 2:11.}

Why do you seek any other path to glory, but that in which you are called to follow the "Captain of your Salvation?" The life of Christ was a continual cross, and desirest thou a perpetuity of repose and joy? Know, therefore, your life must be a continual death to the appetites and passions of fallen nature: and know also that the more perfectly you die to yourself, the more truly will you begin to live to God; if you would then enjoy true peace here, and obtain hereafter the unfading crown of glory, it is necessary that in every place, and in all events, you should bear the cross willingly. To suffer, therefore, is your portion; and to suffer patiently, and willingly, is the great testimony of your love and allegiance to your Lord.

Prepare then your spirit to suffer patiently the many inconveniences and troubles of this life; for these you will find, and can never avoid, though you run to the ends of the earth, or hide yourself in its deepest caverns; and it is patient suffering only that can either disarm their power, or heal the wounds they have made. But while every tribulation is painful and grievous, and it is the desire of your soul to avoid it, you cannot but be wretched; and what you labour to shun will follow you wherever you go. The patient enduring of the cross, and the death of the self upon it, are the indispensable duty of fallen man: and it is thus only, he can be delivered from his darkness, corruption, and misery, and be restored to the possession of life, light, and peace.

Having then no other desire, but that of ardently reaching after Him, of dwelling ever with Him, and of sinking into nothingness before Him, we should accept indiscriminately all His dispensations, whether obscurity or illumination, fruitfulness or barrenness, weakness or strength, sweetness or bitterness, temptations, wanderings, pain, weariness, or doubtings; and none of all these should retard our course.

Chapter 10

On Mortification

All endeavours merely to rectify the exterior, impel the soul yet farther outward into that about which it is so warmly and zealously engaged; and thus its powers are diffused and scattered abroad; for its application being immediately directed to externals, it thus invigorates those very senses it is aiming to subdue.

This species of mortification can never subdue the passions, or lesson their activity. The only method to effect this, is inward silence; by which the soul is turned, wholly and altogether inward, to possess a Present God. If it direct all its vigour and energy towards this centre of its being, the simple act separates and withdraws it from the senses; the excercising of all its powers internally, leaves the senses faint and impotent; and the nearer it draws to God, the farther is it separated from the senses, and the less are the passions influenced by them.

In the mortification of the eye and ear, which continually supply the busy imagination with new subjects, there is little danger of falling into excess: God will teach us this, and we have only to follow where his Spirit guides.

The soul has a double advantage by proceeding thus: for, in withdrawing from outward objects, it draws the nearer to God; and the nearer its approaches are made to Him, besides the secret sustaining power and virtue it receives, it is farther removed from sin: so that at length, to have the mind turned to God, becomes, as it were, habitual.

Chapter 11

On Resignation

We should give up our whole existence unto God, from the strong and positive conviction, that while we are faithfully endeavouring to follow Him, the occurrence of every moment is agreeable to His immediate will and permission, and just such as our state requires. This conviction will make us resigned in all things; and accept of all that happens, not as from the creature, but as from God Himself.

But I entreat you, who sincerely wish to give up yourselves to God, that after you have made the donation, you will not snatch yourselves back again; remember, a gift once presented, is no longer at the disposal of the donor. Resignation is a matter of the greatest importance in our progress; it is the key to the inner court; so that whosoever knows truly how to resign himself, soon becomes perfect: we must, therefore, continue steadfast and immovable therein; and not listen to the voice of natural reason. Great faith produces great resignation: we must confide in God, "hoping against hope." (Romans 4:18.)

Resignation is casting off all selfish care, that we may be altogether at the Divine disposal. All Christians are exhorted to resignation; for it is said to all: Be not anxious for to-morrow; for your Heavenly Father knoweth all that is necessary for you. (Matthew 6:32, 34.) "In all thy ways acknowledge Him, and He shall direct thy paths." (Proverbs 3:6.) "Commit thy works unto the Lord, and thy thoughts shall be established." (Proverbs 16:3.) "Commit thy way unto the Lord, trust also in Him, and He shall bring it to pass; and he shall bring forth thy righteousness as the light, and thy judgment as the noon-day." (Psalm 37:5, 6.)

This virtue is practised by continually losing our own will in the will of God; by being resigned in all things, leaving what is past, in oblivion, what is to come, after having faithfully done our part, to the direction of God, and devoting the present moment to Him, by attributing nothing that befalls us to the creature, but regarding all things in God, and looking upon all, excepting only our sins, as infallibly proceeding from Him. Surrender yourselves, then, to be led and disposed of, just as God pleaseth.

We must willingly co-operate with, and second, the designs of God; which tend to divest us of all our own operations, that in the place thereof His may be instituted. Let this, then, be done in you; and suffer not yourself to be attached to any thing, however good it may appear; for it is no longer good, if it in any measure turns you aside from that which God willeth of you.

The Divine Will is preferable to all things else. And it is our conformity to this sweet yoke that introduces us into the regions of internal peace. Hence we may know that the rebellion of our will is the chief occasion of all our disquiet, and that this is the cause why we suffer so many straights and perturbations. Oh! if we did but submit our wills to the Divine will, and to all its disposals, what tranqillity should we feel! what sweet peace! what inward serenity! what supreme felicity, and foretastes of blessedness! Let us shake off, then, all attachment to the interests of self, and live on Faith and Resignation alone.

Chapter 12

On Virtue

It is thus that we acquire virtue with facility and certainty; for as God is the fountain and principle of all virtue, in proportion as we approach to the possession of Him, in like proportion do we rise into the most eminent virtues. Indeed, he that hath God, hath all things; and he that hath Him not, hath nothing. All virtue is but as a mask, an outside appearance, mutable as our garments, if it does not spring up from this Divine source; and then, indeed, it is genuine, essential, and permanent: "The King's daughter," saith David, "is all glorious within." (Psalm 45:13.)

Chapter 13

On Conversion

"Turn ye, turn ye from your evil ways, for why will ye die, O house of Israel?" (Ezekiel 33:11.) "Turn ye unto Him from whom ye have deeply revolted." (Isaiah 31:6.) To be truly converted, is to avert wholly from the creature, and turn wholly unto God.

For the attainment of salvation, it is absolutely necessary that we should forsake outward sin, and turn unto righteousness: but this alone is not perfect conversion, which consists in a total change of the whole man, from an outward to an inward life.

When the soul is once turned to God, it finds a wonderful facility in continuing steadfast in its conversion; and the longer it remains thus converted, the nearer it approaches, and the more firmly it adheres to God; and the nearer it draws to Him, of necessity, the farther it is removed from that spirit, which is contrary to Him: thus the soul is so effectually established and rooted in its conversion, that a state of conversion becomes in some measure natural to it.

Now, we must not suppose, that this is effected by a violent exertion of its own powers; for the soul is not capable of, nor should it attempt, any other co-operation with Divine Grace, than that of endeavouring to withdraw itself from external objects, and to turn inward; after which, it has nothing farther to do, than to continue steadfast in its adherence to God.

God has an attractive virtue, which draws the soul more and more powerfully to Himself, the nearer it approaches towards Him, and in attracting, he purifies and refines it; just as it is with a gross vapour exhaled by the sun, which, as it gradually ascends, is rarified and rendered pure: the vapour, indeed, contributes to its exhalation only by its passiveness; but the soul co-operates with the attractions of its God, by a free and affectionate correspondence. This turning of the mind inward is both easy and efficacious, advancing the soul naturally, and without constraint, because God Himself is the centre which attracts it.

All our care and attention should therefore be, to acquire inward silence: nor let us be discouraged by the pains and difficulties we encounter in this exercise, which will soon be recompensed on the part of our God, by such abundant supplies of His strength as will render the exercise perfectly easy, provided we are faithful in meekly withdrawing our hearts from outward objects and gratifications, and returning to our centre, with affections full of tenderness and serenity. When at any time the passions are turbulent, a gentle retreat inward unto a present God, easily deadens and pacifies them; and any other way of contending with them, rather irritates than appeases them. One word of our Saviour, in time past, instantly calmed a boisterous and raging sea {Mark 4:35-41, Luke 8:22-25, Matthew 8:23-27}; and can we now doubt, if we sincerely apply to Him in our distress, that He would still the tumults of the agitated soul?

Chapter 14

On Self-Annihilation

The soul becomes fitted for union with God, by giving up Self to the destroying and annihilating power of Divine Love. This, indeed, is a most essential and necessary sacrifice in the Christian religion, and that only by which we pay true homage to the sovereignty of God. By the destruction of the existence of Self within us, we truly acknowledge the supreme existence of our God; for unless we cease to exist in Self, the Spirit of the Eternal Word cannot exist in us. Now it is by the giving up of our own life, that we give place for His coming and, in dying to ourselves, He Himself liveth and abideth in us. (Galatians 2:20.)

We should, indeed, surrender our whole being unto Christ Jesus; and cease to live any longer in ourselves, that He Himself may become our life; "that being dead, our life may be hid with Christ in God." (Colossians 3:3.) By leaving and forsaking ourselves we are lost in Him; and this can be effected only by the annihilation of Self, which being the true prayer of adoration, renders unto "God, and unto the Lamb, blessing, and honour, and glory, and power, for ever and ever!" (Revelation 5:13.)

This is the Prayer of Truth; "It is worshipping God in spirit and in truth:" (John 4:23) because we here come to know the spirit to help our infirmities, and make intercession for us (Romans 8:26); and being thus influenced by the pure Spirit of God, we are thereby drawn forth and freed from our own carnal and corrupt manner of praying. We can pay due honour to God only in our own annihilation; which is no sooner accomplished, than He who never suffers a void in nature, instantly fills us with Himself.

Did we but know the virtues and the blessings which the soul derives from this species of prayer, we should willingly be employed therein without ceasing. It is the pearl of great price; it is the hidden treasure (Matthew 13:44, 46); which, whoever findeth, selleth all that he hath to purchase it; It is the "well of living water, which springeth up into everlasting life" (John 4:14): It is the true adoration of God and comprehends the full performance of the purest evangelical precepts.

Jesus Christ assureth us, that the "Kingdom of God is within us" (Luke 17:21); and this is true in two senses: First, God becometh so fully the Master and Lord in us, that nothing resisteth His dominion: then is our interior His kingdom. And again, when we possess God, who is the supreme Good, we possess His kingdom also, wherein there is fullness of joy and where we attain the end of our creation. The end of our creation, indeed, is to enjoy our God, even in this life; but, alas! how few there are who ever come to know the pure joy which His Presence gives.

Chapter 15

Man Acts More Nobly Under the Divine Influence, Than He Can Possibly Do by Following His Own Will.

Some persons, when they hear of the prayer of silence, falsely imagine that the soul remains dead and inactive; but, unquestionably, it acteth therein, more nobly and more extensively than it had ever done before; for God Himself is its mover, and it now acteth by the agency of His Spirit. When St. Paul speaks of our being led by the Spirit of God, it is not meant that we should cease from action; but that we should act through the internal agency of His grace. This is finely represented by the prophet Ezekiel's vision of the wheels, which had a Living Spirit; and whithersoever the Spirit was to go, they went; they ascended, and descended as they were moved: for the Spirit of Life was in them, and they turned not when they went. (Ezekiel 1:15-21.) Thus the soul should be equally subservient to the will of that vivifying Spirit wherewith it is enlightened, and scrupulously faithful to follow only as that moves. Our activity should, therefore, consist in endeavouring to acquire and maintain such a state, as may be most susceptible of Divine impressions, most flexible to all the operations of the Eternal Word.

Whilst a tablet is unsteady, the painter is unable to delineate a true copy: so every act of our own selfish spirit, is productive of false and erroneous lineaments; it interrupts the work, and defeats the design, of this adorable painter: we must then remain in peace, and move only when he moves us. Jesus Christ hath The Life in Himself (John 5:26), and He is the life of every living soul.

As all action is estimable only in proportion to the dignity of the efficient principle, this action is incontestably more noble than any other. Actions produced by a Divine principle, are Divine; but creaturely actions, however good they may appear, are only human. Jesus Christ, the Word, hath The Life in Himself; and being communicative of His nature, He desireth to communicate it to man. We should, therefore, make room for the influx of this Life, which can only be done by the ejection of the fallen nature; and the suppression of the activity of Self. This is agreeable to the assertion of St. Paul: "If any man be in Christ, he is a new creature: old things are passed away; behold all things are become new!" (2 Corinthians 5:17.) But this state can be accomplished only by dying to ourselves, and to all our own activity, that the influence of God may be substituted in its stead.

Man may, indeed, open the window; but it is the Sun himself, that must give the Light. Jesus Christ has exemplified this in the Gospel: Martha did what was right; but because she did it in her own spirit, Christ rebuked her. The spirit of man is restless and turbulent; for which reason it does little, though it would appear to do much. "Martha," saith Christ, "Thou art careful, and troubled about many things; but one thing is needful; and Mary hath chosen that good part which shall not be taken away from her." (Luke 10:41, 42.) And what was it that Mary had chosen?   Repose, tranquillity, and peace. She apparently ceased to act, that the Spirit of Christ might act in her; she ceased to live, that Christ might be her life.

St. Peter, in the warmth of his affection, told the Lord, that for His sake he was ready, willingly to lay down his life; but, at the word of a young damsel, he denied Him.

The many troubles in life, come from the soul not abiding in its place, and not being content with the will of God, and what is afforded therein, from time to time. Many souls may be resigned as to the general will, and yet fail as to the present moment: being out of the will of God, they fall; they renew such falls, as long as they continue out of the Divine will; when they return into it, all will go on well. God loves what is done in His own order, and of His own will and time; and while you faithfully give yourself up thereto, you will do all things right.

All men have more or less of ardent desires, except those who live in the Divine will. Some of these desires may appear to be good; but unless they be according to the will of God, he who rests in the Divine will, though he be exempt from all these desires, is infinitely more peaceful, and glorifies God more. This shows us how necessary it is to renounce ourselves, and all our own activity, to follow Christ Jesus; and we cannot follow Him, without being animated with His Spirit. Now that His Spirit may gain admission in us, it is necessary, that our own spirit should be first subdued: "He that is joined unto the Lord," saith St. Paul, "is one Spirit." (1 Corinthians 6:17.)

All things should be done in their season {Ecclesiastes 3:1}: every state has its commencement, its progress, and its consummation; and it is an unhappy error to stop in the beginning. There is even no art but what has its process; and at first we must labour with diligence and toil, but at last we shall reap the harvest of our industry. When the vessel is in port, the mariners are obliged to exert all their strength that they may clear her thence, and put to sea; but at length they turn her with facility, as they please. In like manner, while the soul remains in sin and creaturely entanglements, very frequent and strenuous endeavours, are requisite to effect its freedom; the cords which hold it must be loosed; and then, by strong and vigorous efforts, it pushes off gradually from its old port; and, in leaving that at a distance, it proceeds to the haven to which it wishes to steer.

When the vessel is thus put in motion, in proportion as she advances on the sea, she leaves the land behind; and the farther she departs from the old harbour, the less difficulty and labour is requisite in moving her forward: at length she begins to get sweetly under sail; and now proceeds so swiftly in her course, that the oar, which is become useless, is laid aside. How is the Pilot now employed? He is content with spreading the sails, and holding the rudder. To spread the sails, is to lay the mind open before God, that it may be acted upon by His Spirit; to hold the rudder, is to restrain the heart from wandering from the true course, recalling it gently and guiding it steadily to the dictates of the Blessed Spirit, which gradually gain possession and dominion of it; just as the wind by degrees fills the sails, and impels the vessel.

While the winds are fair, the mariners rest from their labours, and the vessel glides rapidly along without their toil; and when they thus repose, and leave the vessel to the wind, they make more way in one hour, than they had done in a length of time by all their former efforts: were they now even to attempt using the oar, they would not only fatigue themselves, but retard the vessel by their illtimed labours.

This is the manner of acting we should pursue interiorly; it will, indeed, advance us in a very short time, by the Divine influence, infinitely farther than a whole life spent in reiterated acts of self-exertion; and whosoever will take this path, will find it easier than any other.

If the wind be contrary and blow a storm instead of putting out to sea, we must cast anchor to hold the vessel. Our anchor is a firm confidence and hope in God, waiting patiently the calming of the tempest, and the return of a more favourable gale, as David "waited patiently for the Lord, and He inclined unto him, and heard his cry." (Psalm 40:1.) We must, therefore, be resigned to the Spirit of God, giving up ourselves wholly to His divine guidance; never suffering ourselves to be disquieted by any accident; for inquietude is the door by which the enemy gets into the soul, to rob it of its peace: neither should we concern, or busy ourselves, with what others say and do, for this will be a great cause of disturbance to us.

Let us pacify all the motions of our heart, as soon as we see it in agitation. Let us quit all pleasure that comes not from God alone. Let us do away all unprofitable thoughts and musings. Let us diligently seek God within us, and we shall infallibly find Him, and with Him, joy and peace; such joy and peace as will endure in the midst of suffering, and which, flowing from an inexhaustible source, become a perpetual fountain of delight. "Peace I leave with you," said Christ to His followers, "my peace I give unto you, not as the world giveth, give I unto you." (John 14:27.)

Did we but know the blessedness of hearkening unto God, and how greatly the soul is strengthened and invigorated thereby, all flesh would surely be silent before the Lord (Zechariah 2:13); all would be still, as soon as He appeareth. But to engage us further in a boundless resignation, God assures us, by the same Prophet, that we should fear nothing in thus giving up ourselves to Him, because He takes care of us, surpassing the highest tenderness of which we can form an idea: "Can a woman," saith He, "forget her sucking child, that she should not have compassion on the son of her womb? Yea, she may forget; yet will I not forget thee." (Isaiah 49:15.) Oh blessed assurance, full of consolation! Who, after this, shall be fearful of resigning themselves wholly to the dispensation and guidance of their God!

All men seek for peace, but they seek where it is not to be found. They seek it in the world, which is ever promising, but can never give us solid peace; for, wherever we go, we shall carry this fruitful source of every perplexity, our own unsubdued and selfish will. The love of liberty is one of the most dangerous passions of the heart. If we follow this propensity, instead of true liberty, it reduces us to slavery. As our passions are the worst of our tyrants, if we obey them partially, we must always be in a perpetual strife and contest within; and if we entirely give ourselves up to them, it is horrid to think to what extremities they will lead; they will torment the heart, and, like a torrent, sweep all before them, and yet never be satisfied. True liberty is to be found only in Him, whose truth shall set us free (John

8:3?), and who shall make us experience, that to serve Him is to reign.

That piety by which we are sanctified, and entirely devoted to God, consists in doing His will precisely in all circumstances of life. Take what steps you please, do what deeds you will, let them shine with lustre, yet you shall not be rewarded, but for having done the will of your Sovereign Master. Although your servant did wonders in your house, yet if he did not what you required, you would not value his service, and you might justly complain of him as a bad servant.

There is no good spirit but that of God {Luke 18:19}: that spirit which removes us from the true good, is but a spirit of illusion, however flattering it may appear. Who would be carried in a magnificent chariot on the road to an abyss! The way which leads to a precipice is frightful, although it should be covered with roses; but the way that leads to a crown is delightful, although it should be thick set with thorns. He has given His good Spirit to instruct us (Nehemia 9:20), therefore, let us no longer follow our own will but His; so that not only our religious actions, but also all others, may be done with no other view but that of pleasing Him: then will our whole conduct be sanctified; then will our deeds become a continual sacrifice; and incessant prayer, and uninterrupted love, will occupy the heart: therefore, let us submit to the annihilation of our own will, that His will may reign in us! For it is His prerogative to command, and our duty to obey.

Chapter 16

On the Possession of Peace and Rest before God

The soul that is faithful in the exercise of that love and adherence to God already described, is astonished to feel Him gradually taking possession of its whole being; and now enjoys a continual sense of that Presence, which is become as it were natural to it. The Presence of God diffuses an unusual serenity throughout all our faculties – it calms the mind, and gives sweet repose and quiet even in the midst of our daily labours; but then we must be resigned to Him without reserve.

We must however urge it as a matter of the highest importance, to cease from self-action and self-exertion, that God Himself may act alone: He saith by the mouth of His Prophet David, "Be still, and know that I am God." (Psalm 46:10.) Yet those greatly err, who accuse this species of prayer of idleness, a charge that can only arise from inexperience. If they would but make some efforts towards the attainment of it, they would soon experience the contrary of what they suppose, and find their accusation groundless.

This appearance of inaction is, indeed, not the consequence of sterility and want, but of fruitfulness and abundance; this will be clearly perceived by the experienced soul, which will know and feel, that its silence is full and unctuous, and the result of causes totally the reverse of apathy and barrenness. The interior is not a strong hold, to be taken by storm and violence; but a kingdom of Peace, which is to be gained only by Love. Let us then give ourselves up to God without apprehension of danger. He will love us, and enable us to love Him; and that love, increasing daily, will produce in us all other virtues. He alone can replenish our hearts which the world has agitated and intoxicated, but never could fill.

He will take nothing from us but what makes us unhappy. He will only make us despise the world, which we do perhaps already. We shall only be made to alter a little in our actions, and correct the motive of them, by making all referrible to Him. Then the most ordinary and seemingly indifferent actions will become exercises of virtue, and sources of consolation. We shall behold in peace the approach of death, as the beginning of life immortal, and as St. Paul saith, "we shall not be uncloathed; but cloathed upon, and mortality shall be swallowed up of life." (2 Corinthians 5:4.)

Let us therefore no longer fear to commit ourselves wholly to God. What risk do we run, in depending solely on Him! Ah! He will not deceive us, unless by bestowing an abundance beyond our highest hopes: but those who expect all from themselves, will inevitably be deceived, and must suffer this rebuke of God by His prophet Isaiah: "Behold all ye that kindle a fire, that compass yourselves about with sparks; walk in the light of your fire, and in the sparks that ye have kindled. This shall ye have of mine hand, ye shall lie down in sorrow." (Isaiah 50:11.)

The soul advanced thus far, hath no need of any other preparative than its quietude; for now the Presence of God, which is the great effect, or rather continuation of Prayer, begins to be powerfully felt, and the soul experiences what the Apostle Paul saith, that "Eye hath not seen, nor ear heard, neither have entered into the heart of man, the things which God hath prepared for them that love Him." (1 Corinthians 2:9.) The soul certainly enjoys transcendent blessedness, and feels that it is no longer she that lives, but Christ that liveth in her (Galatians 2:20); and that the only way to find Him is to turn the mind inward. We no sooner do this, than we are filled with the consolations of His Presence: we are amazed at so great a blessing, and enjoy an internal converse, which external matters cannot interrupt.

The same may be said of this species of prayer, that is said of wisdom: "All good things come together with her." (Wisdom 7:11.) For the virtues now flow from us into action with so much sweetness and facility, that they appear natural and spontaneous.

Chapter 17

On Perfection, or the Union of the Soul with God

The most profitable and desirable state in this life, is that of Christian perfection, which consists in the union of the soul with God, a union that includes in it all spiritual good; producing in us a wonderful freedom of spirit, which raises us above all the events and changes of this life, and which frees us from the tyranny of human fear; it gives an extraordinary power for the well performing all our actions, and acquitting ourselves well in our employments; a prudence truly Christian in all our undertakings; a peace and perfect tranquillity in all conditions; and, in short, a continual victory over self-love and our passions.

It is impossible to attain Divine Union, solely by the activity of meditation, or by the meltings of the affections, or even by the highest degree of luminous and elegantly composed prayer; for, according to Scripture, "no man shall see God and live." (Exodus 33:20.) Now all the exercises of discoursive prayer, and even of active contemplation, being performed in the *life* of our own will, we "cannot thereby see God;" for all that is of man's own power or exertion, must first die, be it ever so noble, ever so exalted.

St. John relates, "that there was silence in heaven" (Revelation 8:1): Now heaven represents the centre of the soul, wherein, ere the majesty of God appears, all must be hushed to silence. All the efforts, nay the very existence of Self-love must be destroyed: because it is the natural will that is opposed to God, and all the malignity of man proceeds from it, insomuch that the purity of a soul increases, in proportion as the natural will becomes subjected to the Divine Will.

Therefore, the soul can never arrive at Divine Union but by the annihilation of its will; nor can it ever become one with God, but by being re-established in the purity of its first creation. God purifies the soul by His Wisdom, as refiners do metals in the furnace. Gold cannot be purified but by fire, which gradually separates from it, and consumes, all that is earthly and heterogeneous: it must be melted and dissolved, and all impure mixtures taken away, by casting it again and again into the furnace: thus it is refined from all internal corruption, and even exalted to a state incapable of farther purification. It now no longer contains any adulterate mixture; its purity is perfect, its simplicity complete; and it is fit for the most exquisite workmanship. Thus we may see that the Divine Spirit, as an unremitting fire, must devour and destroy all that is earthly, sensual, and carnal, and all self-activity, before the soul can be fitted for, and capable of union with God.

"I will make a man more precious than Gold." (Isaiah 13:12.) But when God begins to burn, destroy, and purify, then the soul, not perceiving the salutary designs of these operations, shrinks from them; and as the gold seems rather to blacken than brighten when first put into the furnace, so the soul conceives that its purity is lost, and that its temptations are its sins.

But while we confess, that the enjoyment of God is the end for which we were created; that "without holiness" (Hebrews 12:14) none can attain it; and, that to attain it, we must necessarily pass through a severe and purifying process; how strange is it, that we should dread and avoid this process, as if that could be the cause of evil and imperfection in the present life, which is to be productive of glory and blessedness in the life to come!

Let all, then, press forward towards the mark, suffering themselves to be guided and governed by the Spirit of Grace, which would infallibly conduct them to the end of their creation, the enjoyment of God.

It may perhaps be said, that some may feign to have attained this blessed state; but, alas! none can any more feign this, than the wretch, who is on the point of perishing with hunger, can for a length of time feign to be full and satisfied: some wish or word, some sigh or sign, will inevitably escape him, and betray his famished state.

"Be ye perfect, even as your Father which is in heaven is perfect." (Matthew 5:48.) The soul remaining in its disorderly will, is imperfect; it becomes more perfect, in proportion as it approaches nearer to the will of God. When a soul is advanced so far, that it cannot in any thing depart from the Divine will, it then becomes wholly perfect, united with, and transformed into the Divine nature; and being thus purified and united to God, it finds a profound peace, and a sweet rest, which brings it to such a perfect union of love, that it is filled with joy. It conforms itself to the will of its God in all emergencies, and rejoices in every thing to do Divine good pleasure.

The Lord draws near to such a soul, and communicates Himself inwardly to it. He fills it with Himself because it is empty, clothes it with His light and with His love, because it is naked; lifts it up because it is low; and unites it with Himself.

If you would enter into this heaven on earth, forget every care and every anxious thought, get out of yourself that the love of God may live in your soul; so that you may be enabled to say with the Apostle: "I live, yet not I, but Christ liveth in me." (Galatians 2:20.) How happy should we be if we could thus leave all for God, seek Him only, breathe after none but Him; let Him only have our sighs! O, that we could but go on without interruption, towards the enjoyment of this blessed state! God calls us thereto. He invites us to enter into our inward centre, where He will renew and change us, and show us a new and heavenly kingdom, full of joy, peace, content and serenity.

The spiritual, abstracted, and retired soul hath here its peace no more broken, though outwardly it may meet with combats, and may sometimes be naked, forsaken, fought against, and desolate, because from the infinite distance, tempests never reach to that serenest heaven within, where pure and perfect love resides. For, although the prince of darkness may indeed make violent assaults against it;

yet it makes head against them, and stands like a strong pillar; no more happening to it, than happens to a high mountain in a storm. The valley is darkened with thick clouds, fierce tempests of hail, and thunder; while the lofty mountain glitters by the bright beams of the sun, in quietness and serenity, continuing clear like heaven, immoveable, and full of light: such a soul, indeed, is, as "mount Zion which cannot be removed, but abideth for ever." (Psalm 125:1.)

In this throne of quiet, are manifest the perfections of spiritual beauty: here we shall enjoy the true light of the secret and divine mysteries of Christ, perfect humility, the amplest resignation, the meekness and innocency of the dove, liberty and purity of heart; here is witnessed joyful simplicity, heavenly indifferency, continual prayer, a total nakedness, perfect disinterestedness, a conversation of heaven.

This is the rich and hidden treasure; this is the pearl of great price.

FINIS.

CPSIA information can be obtained
at www.ICGtesting.com
Printed in the USA
LVOW01s1935090616
491954LV00034B/649/P